101 THINGS
TO TAKE THE STRESS OUT OF CHRISTMAS

101 THINGS
TO TAKE THE STRESS OUT OF CHRISTMAS

ROBIN SNOW

Published in the UK in 2017 by Short Books
Unit 316, ScreenWorks,
22 Highbury Grove, London N5 2ER

10 9 8 7 6 5 4 3 2 1

A CIP catalogue record for this book is available from the British Library.

ISBN 978-1-78072-329-7

Printed and bound in Great Britain by
CPI Group (UK) Ltd, Croydon, CR0 4YY

Page layouts by Paul Bougourd
Cover design by Two Associates

Introduction

If you're reading this then you've noticed it too. Christmas is billed as white snow, delicious meals and *Love, Actually* – but it can all too easily end up being the *stress*-tive season, your best laid plans scuppered by disappointed children, mess everywhere and too much heat in the kitchen.

It doesn't have to be this way. Christmas should be as fun as it was when you were a child. And with this book it can be!

So put on that cosy jumper, don those novelty reindeer antlers, and flick through these pages full of delightful games, activities and tips to help you feel festive and full of joy!

1.

Move Christmas to January this year.

2.

Compile a playlist of your favourite festive tunes.

What are your five essential tracks?

1 ....

....

2 ....

....

3 ....

....

4 ....

....

5 ....

....

3.

Mix up a snowball:

First smear the juice of a lime around the rim of the glass and dip it into some coconut flakes.

Load up your glass with ice and fill to half way with lemonade. Squeeze in the juice of half a lime and top up the rest of the glass with advocaat.

4.

Complete these festive words:

1. T__K_Y B_ST_R
2. _AC_ F__S_
3. CH__S__A_ _R_E
4. B_U__E_ _PR__T
5. M_ST__T_E
6. F__H_R _HR__T__S
7. A__E_T C__E_D_R
8. _NO__L_K_S

Festive word solutions:

1. TURKEY BASTER
2. JACK FROST
3. CHRISTMAS TREE
4. BRUSSEL SPROUT
5. MISTLETOE
6. FATHER CHRISTMAS
7. ADVENT CALENDAR
8. SNOWFLAKES

5.

Paint your fingernails with Christmas decorations.

6.

Try to remember one present you received from each of your last 5 Christmases.

Year	Gift

See? They're not that important after all.

7.

Play "Spot the ISS".

See how many times you can spot the International Space Station over the Christmas holidays. Can you beat your friends and family?

Go to: spotthestation.nasa.gov

(If nothing else it's an excuse to while away the time looking at the stars.)

8.

Keep it simple.

Buy the same gift for everyone you know...

9.

...or, alternatively, buy all your presents in one trip to the local charity shop.

10.

Design your dream Christmas jumper.

11.

Start a street competition for the house with the best lights display.

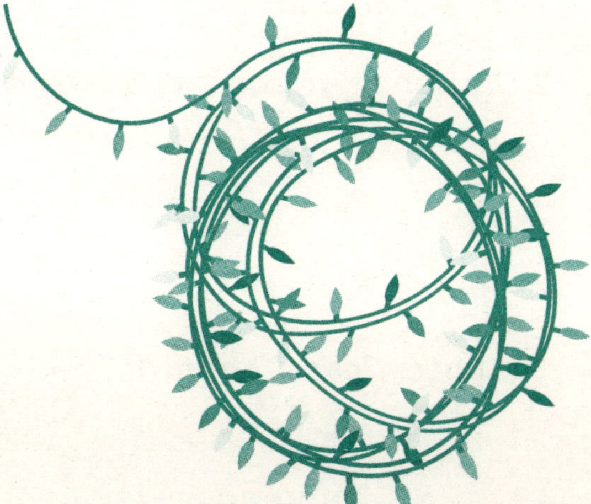

12.

Can you match up the famous quotes opposite with the Christmas movies below?

1. *It's a Wonderful Life*
2. *National Lampoon's Christmas Vacation*
3. *Elf*
4. *Miracle on 34th Street*
5. *Santa Claus: The Movie*

Answers: 1c, 2e, 3a, 4b, 5d

a) "I passed through the seven levels of the Candy Cane forest, through the sea of swirly twirly gum drops, and then I walked through the Lincoln Tunnel."

b) "Well, I would greatly like to oblige, Mr. Collins, but I cannot make this reindeer fly."

c) "Teacher says every time a bell rings an angel gets his wings."

d) "A sequel. That's it. We'll bring it out on March 25, and we'll call it... Christmas 2!"

e) "Can I refill your eggnog for you? Get you something to eat? Drive you out to the middle of nowhere and leave you for dead?"

13.

Get crafty!

Make christmas decorations with fir cones and dried orange segments.

14.

Hibernate for the festive season.

15.

Buy a pint for all the regulars down the pub.

16.

See if you can name all of Santa's reindeer.

(Tip: there are nine of them — including the one with the bright red nose.)

17.

Make your own Christmas cards for printing up.

Find an old family picture, customise it by giving everyone antlers or a Christmas hat and, most importantly, have your names and festive message printed inside, so you don't actually have to write anything.

Happy Christmas!

Yours lazily,
The whole family

18.

Instead of rushing around doing the Christmas shopping, go into town, sit on a bench and just soak up the festive atmosphere.

19.

Reach out to a friend you've lost contact with.

Wish them a Happy Christmas.

20. Create a new Christmas character.

How about Simon the Christmas spider, who leaves sweets in his web?

Or Kelly the Kangaroo, who steals away presents in her pouch?

21

Think back over your family Christmas traditions.

Which one is your favourite?

How did it start?

Do you remember the first time you did it?

22.

Make your own Christmas crackers.

Put in some quirky "treats" or make up your own cheesy jokes.

23.

Do you know the reason why...?

1. We decorate Christmas trees.
2. Boxing Day is called "Boxing Day".
3. Christmas Day is on 25th December.

4. Santa comes down the chimney.
5. We put a penny in the pudding.

24.

Festive wordsearch!

C	A	R	D	P	A	R	T	Y
R	E	L	V	E	S	O	C	D
A	N	L	B	A	M	B	G	D
C	I	R	E	C	E	I	V	E
K	W	J	W	B	R	N	H	L
E	I	O	J	T	R	E	E	L
R	N	Y	F	A	Y	A	K	U
S	M	I	T	Y	N	I	T	M
L	G	S	P	R	O	U	T	E

25.

Plot Santa's most efficient route around the globe on Christmas Eve.

26.

Start a morning jogging routine.

Running is known to be a great stress-buster; it releases endorphins and generally makes you feel good.

27.

Remember that Hugh Grant dance from *Love, Actually*?

Put on your favourite tune and let the music take you!

28.

Take a break from it all by colouring in this Christmassy scene.

29.

Plant a
Christmas rose.

30.

Plan a vegan Christmas Day.

Whole Roasted Cauliflower

Quinoa Nut Roast

Chestnut and Sage Wellington

Carrot Sticks and Dip

Beetroot and Apple Salad Pots

...Then celebrate that you don't actually have to do it!

31.

Play the children's version of Trivial Pursuit to make you all feel a bit smarter.

32.

Make your present wishlist only charitable donations.

1. *Sponsor a dolphin*
2. *Donation to UNICEF*
3. *Volunteer for one afternoon collecting litter*
4. *Have a whip-round for a wetsuit for uncle Dave's cross-channel swim.*

33.

Memorise these historical events, which all happened on Christmas days past.

(It'll ease the stress of starting conversations at the Christmas party.)

800

Coronation of Charlemagne as Holy Roman Emperor.

1066

William the Conqueror crowned King of England.

1642

Sir Isaac Newton born.

1758

Halley's comet visible from Earth.

1922

Vladimir Lenin dictates his "political testament".

1959

Ringo Starr given his first drum kit.

1968

Apollo 8 orbits the moon.

1991

Mikhail Gorbachev resigns as President of USSR.

34.

Write your own carol for the festive season.

Think robins, holly, bells and — of course — snow. Is Santa going to make an appearance? Will your song be religious, or just about getting together with family?

If you can’t think of a melody, rewrite the lyrics to an existing carol.

My carol

Author: ______________________

Date: ______________________

35.

Hosting a Christmas party?

Make it fancy dress, with the theme to be announced on the morning of the party.

Benefits:

- Nobody has time for one-upmanship.
- Seeing how others lose their heads in a stressful situation can only make you feel better.

36.

Go on!
Have an extra-long lie in tomorrow!

37.

Spread joy to the world!

Learn how to say "Merry Christmas" in different languages:

Italian: "Buon Natale!"

Dutch: "Prettig Kerstmis!"

Welsh: "Nadolig Llawen!"

German: "Frohe Weihnachten!"

French: "Joyeux Noël!"

Spanish: "¡Feliz Navidad!"

38.

Make a list of your five favourite things about Christmas and forget about anything else that doesn't make the cut!

1 ....

....

2 ....

....

3 ....

....

4 ....

....

5 ....

....

39.

Don’t bother with the hassle of baking a Christmas cake. Just serve the ingredients instead:

40.

Get yourself some Christmas underwear so you can feel festive from top to toe.

41.

Sequencing quiz.

Put these Christmassy words in their logical order.

(There are no right or wrong answers.)

e.g. Prancer, Dancer, Vixen, Dasher

1st *Dasher* .... 2nd *Dancer* ....

3rd *Prancer* .... 4th *Vixen* ....

1) Snowman, melting, snowfall, sunshine

1st .... 2nd ....

3rd .... 4th ....

2) Calling birds, turtle doves,
a partridge, French hens

1st .... 2nd ....

3rd .... 4th ....

3) Santa, wake, sleep, presents

1st .... 2nd ....

3rd .... 4th ....

4) Blitzen, Donner, Comet, Cupid

1st .... 2nd ....

3rd .... 4th ....

42.

Who is the biggest Grinch you know?

Send them a Christmas card with a personalised message that will make their heart grow three sizes.

43.

Play skittles with your grandparents.
(Or an elderly neighbour.)

44. Spot the difference:

(10 to find)

NORTH POLE

45.

Imagine you are spending Christmas on the other side of the world.

What do you think you'd like about it?

What would you miss?

46.

Compete with the big corporations by writing your own Christmas advert about not spending any extra money over the Christmas period.

You'll need to include:

- A bouncy or mellow pop backing track.
- A warm-hearted message.
- A quirky twist on the norm.

Why not act it out and see if it goes viral online?

47.

Play the sentence game...

1. Think up a selection of strange sentences that you and your family wouldn't usually say. (Or use the suggestions opposite.)
2. Write them on strips of paper, mix them up in a hat and get each player to pick one out at random.
3. Each player keeps their sentence secret, but must drop it into conversation over dinner — and they must say it without others realising it is their sentence.
4. Devise forfeits for anyone who gets caught, or who calls someone out incorrectly.

Some sentence ideas you could use:

"THAT'S SOMETHING THAT DONALD TRUMP AND I WILL ALWAYS AGREE ON."

"THE TRUTH IS, *FIFTY SHADES OF GREY* IS FULL OF REALLY HELPFUL IDEAS."

"FORGET THE STONES OR THE BEATLES, I THINK THE GOODIES WERE THE REAL POP PIONEERS."

"YOU CAN NEVER TRUST A JUGGLER."

"APPARENTLY FROWNING WORKS MORE MUSCLES THAN RUNNING A MARATHON."

48.

No snow?

Make your own
winter wonderland
in your living room...

49.

Take the hassle out of finding love this Christmas.

Nothing says "you'll do" like a dangling mistletoe hat.

50.

Play "Hide the Elf".

A great ongoing game to occupy friends and family.

Cut out the picture on the page opposite and hide it in a different place around the house each day for people to find.

(It's also a good way to remind the kids that they should be good – because Santa's elf is watching!)

51.

Don't wait until New Year — make your resolution now:

Get it out of the way so you can forget about it over Christmas.

52.

Relax by watching a warming video of a crackling Norwegian fire.

Try this one:

https://www.youtube.com/watch?v=g-GWhx68HuI

53.

Take your mind off Christmas with this alphabetical sudoku:

	E		F		I			
	G				B		E	H
A			E			I		
	A	I						E
			G			A		C
	B	F	A		E			
		G					A	
H				F			D	I
B		A	H	D	G			F

The same rules apply, except you must use letters A-I rather than numbers 1-9 to make it that bit more fiendish.

54.

Decorate the tree with biscuits

so you can secretly snack throughout the Christmas period.

55.

Forget stress-inducing "to do" lists and give yourself more frivolous targets.

Try spotting these things when you're out running festive errands:

1. A robin
2. A traffic cone
3. Some elaborate facial hair
4. Something incongruous e.g. a decoration featuring the Easter Bunny
5. Someone doing a good deed

56.

Add a Christmas tradition from a foreign country to your celebrations this year.

Why not try one of these:

<u>Portugal</u>
Set extra places at the breakfast table for deceased relatives.

<u>Catalonia</u>
Add a statuette of a defecating man to the nativity scene.

<u>Ukraine</u>
Decorate your Christmas tree with a fake spider's web.

<u>Norway</u>
Hide away brooms so they are not stolen by witches.

57.

Forget about the things you have to contend with over Christmas, leave the fray...

...and volunteer for a few hours at a soup kitchen.

58.

Knit yourself a Christmas stocking.

Remember, knitting is the ultimate mindfulness activity!

59.

No arguments this year. Make it a household decree that any disagreements must be settled with a Thumb War.

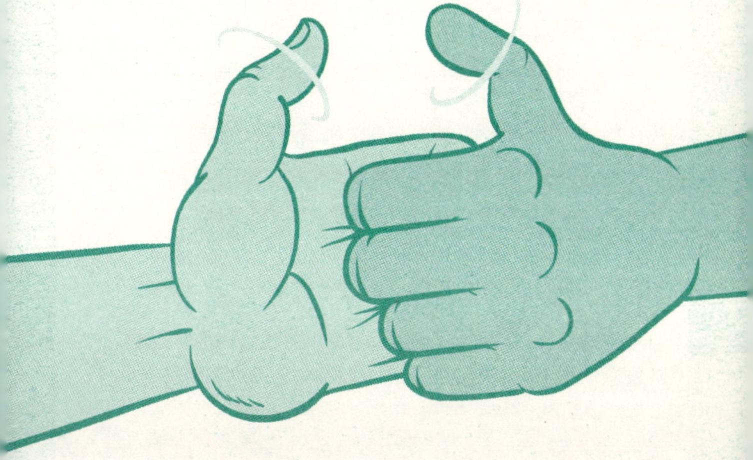

"One, two, three, four,
I declare a Thumb War..."

60

Which people in your life are most like these festive characters:

1. Father Christmas
   (generous to a fault, but will not tolerate bad behaviour)

2. Ebeneezer Scrooge
   (miserly workaholic who just needs guidance to reveal his good spirit)

3. Kevin McAllister in *Home Alone*
   (badly behaved but infinitely resourceful in a tight situation)

4. The Snowman
(doesn't say much despite hidden talents; cold hands, warm heart)

5. Rudolf
(often underappreciated but sometimes just the person to solve a problem)

6. John McLane in *Die Hard*
(not to be messed with but a hopeless romantic at heart; doesn't like to lose)

7. Jack Skellington
(a legendary Goth / Emo music hero for whom Christmas is a guilty pleasure)

8. Buddy the Elf
(eternally youthful, enthusiastic and energetic but impossibly naïve)

61

Recycle your old newspapers and magazines by using them as wrapping paper.

Save your time and money, and save the environment at the same time!

62.

Skip Christmas entirely and go camping in another country.

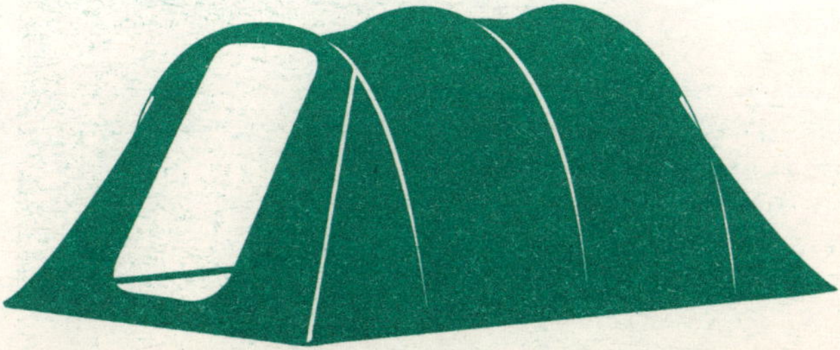

63.

Play your favourite Christmas songs backwards and decode their hidden messages

64.

Invite a guest who has no familial connection but "did not want to be alone at Christmas".

65.

Honour Christmas in your heart by watching as many Dickens adaptations as you can this year.

- ☐ *A Christmas Carol* with Jim Carrey
- ☐ *The Muppet Christmas Carol*
- ☐ *Scrooged* with Bill Murray
- ☐ *Mr Magoo's Christmas Carol*
- ☐ *A Christmas Carol* with George C Scott
- ☐ *A Christmas Carol* with Kelsey Grammer
- ☐ *Blackadder's Christmas Carol*
- ☐ *The Ghost of Girlfriends Past*

66.

Play the matchstick game.

Each player gets dealt 10 matches.

Take it in turns to lay a match on the top of the neck of a bottle.

If you knock any down you must pick them up.

The aim is to be the first to get rid of all of your matches.

67.

Make finger puppets for a finger-puppet nativity.

68.

A happy Christmas
is all about
compromise...

Ban mobile devices
on Christmas Day for
alternate hours only.

Even hours = 

Odd hours = 

69.

Use this napkin folding method for an effortless way to add some style to your dinner table.

(1) Start with a square napkin and fold all four corners into the centre.

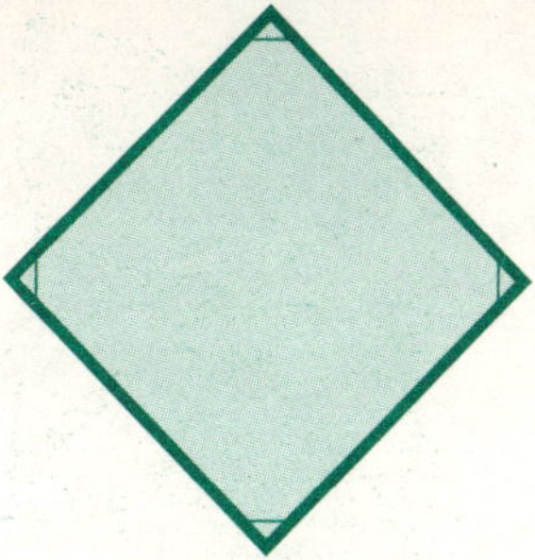

(2) Turn the folded napkin over and again fold all four corners into the centre.

(3) Finally, curl the four corners on the underside up and around to create petal shapes... and voilà!

70.

Bask in nostalgia for yesteryear by trying to remember what you put in your first letter to Father Christmas.

Dear Santa,

....

....

....

....

....

....

....

....

....

71.

Do a really complicated jigsaw puzzle.

And then look forward to that feeling of satisfaction when you put in the last piece.

72.

Give every animal you see a tinsel collar.

...but probably steer clear of the zoo.

73.

Take a slice of Christmas cake to a lonely neighbour and join them for a cup of tea.

74.

Impress your family by reciting this poem on Christmas Day:

Minstrels

by William Wordsworth

The minstrels played their Christmas tune
To-night beneath my cottage-eaves;
While, smitten by a lofty moon,
The encircling laurels, thick with leaves,
Gave back a rich and dazzling sheen,
That overpowered their natural green.

Through hill and valley every breeze
Had sunk to rest with folded wings:
Keen was the air, but could not freeze,
Nor check, the music of the strings;
So stout and hardy were the band
That scraped the chords with strenuous hand.

And who but listened?—till was paid
Respect to every inmate's claim,
The greeting given, the music played
In honour of each household name,
Duly pronounced with lusty call,
And "Merry Christmas" wished to all.

75.

Stocking filler quiz.

The venn diagram below shows which stocking fillers your friends received last year.

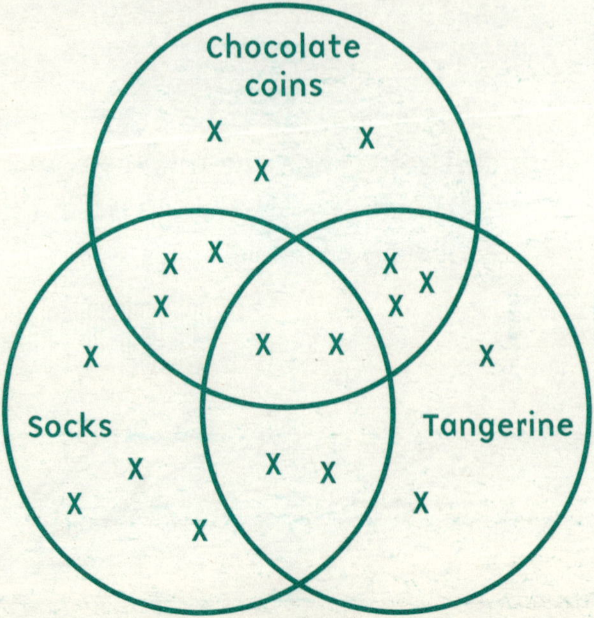

Now answer these questions:

1. How many people didn't get any chocolate?

2. How many people could eat their tangerine knowing they could look forward to some chocolate afterwards?

3. How many people were able to hide their tangerine in a new sock?

4. How many people had to pretend they weren't disappointed at receiving only socks?

5. How many people had a choice about what to eat but had to do so with chilly feet?

76.

Write a Christmas toast to recite before dinner.

77.

Ask your oldest relative to describe Christmas in the old days.

- Where did they spend it?
- And who with?
- What did they do?
- What did it mean to them?

78.

Gobble up Father Christmas's mince pie and glass of whisky.

(Believe me, he's had plenty.)

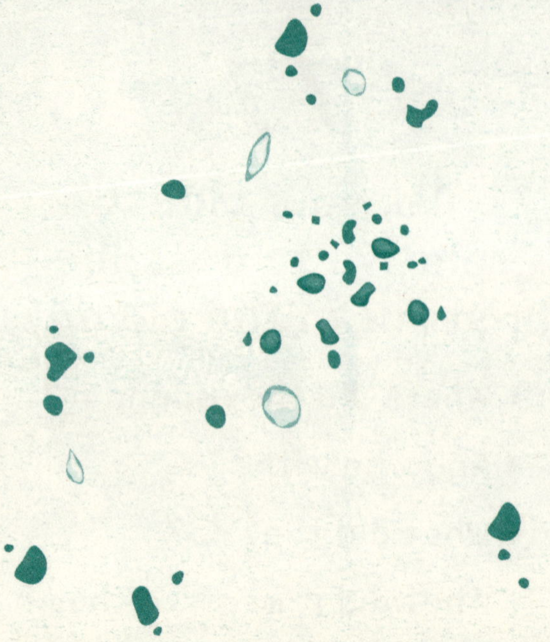

79.

Pick a Christmas song and do the actions it mentions.

Roast chestnuts on an open fire...

Sing Yuletide carols in a choir...

Dress up like eskimos...

Have some turkey...

Hang some mistletoe...

80.

Juggle with the family tin of sweets.

Benefits:

- You'll develop a new skill.
- You'll impress your family.
- It'll take a lot longer to eat through the entire tin.

81.

Don't fret about leftover sprouts.

Here are some further uses for that most underrated of Christmas treats:

- Clear the table and turn them into snooker balls. Use the remaining parsnips as cues.
- Use them as the subject of a still-life illustration class.
- Cover them in melted chocolate for dessert.
- Play "find the sprout"; you only get to open a present when you find one.
- Ceremonially cast them into the garden to rot (and to fertilise the plants).

82.

If you get tired of being festive, bring everyone back to reality with these factoids.

For Santa to give presents to every child who celebrates Christmas:

- He would have to visit 250 million households in one night.
- He would have to travel at over 320 million miles per hour.
- His naughty-or-nice list would be a staggering 14 million pages — that's 13,998,775 pages longer than *War and Peace*!

83.

Kids to entertain?

Get them to design a Christmas poster and give a prize to the winner.

84.

Turn off all the alarm clocks.

No early starts *this* Christmas!

85.

Watch the Queen's speech with your family and friends and play along by doing the following actions:

- Curtsey when she says "we".
- Hug the person to your right when she says "family".
- Salute when she says "United Kingdom" or "Commonwealth".
- Drink when she says "one".
- Cover your ears when she refers to any challenges we face.

You decide how strict the forfeits will be for getting it wrong!

86.

And now write your own Queen's speech reflecting on the year.

Remember: even just writing down your hopes and fears can be a cathartic exercise...

87.

Organise a snap Christmas play, with everyone taking a role, from old to young.

88.

Of course, when you get the family together at Christmas, it's got to be...

Sticky Heads!

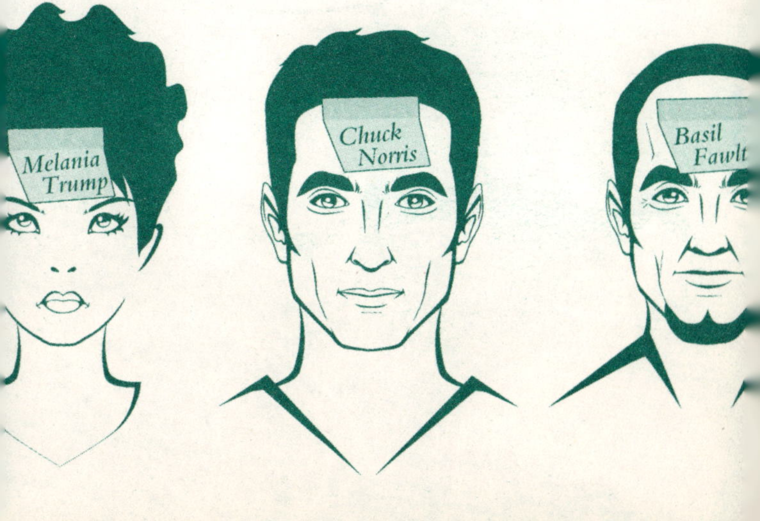

89.

Tot up the calories of your Christmas dinner and feel good about it!

Turkey	= 100 kcal
Stuffing	= 200 kcal
Roast potatoes	= 300 kcal
Pigs in blankets	= 240 kcal
Carrots	= 20 kcal
Green beans	= 15 kcal
Sprouts	= 20 kcal
Christmas pud	= 450 kcal
2 Glasses of wine	= 320 kcal
Total:	Who cares?

90.

Play Scrabble, but spice it up by switching round which letters the tiles represent...

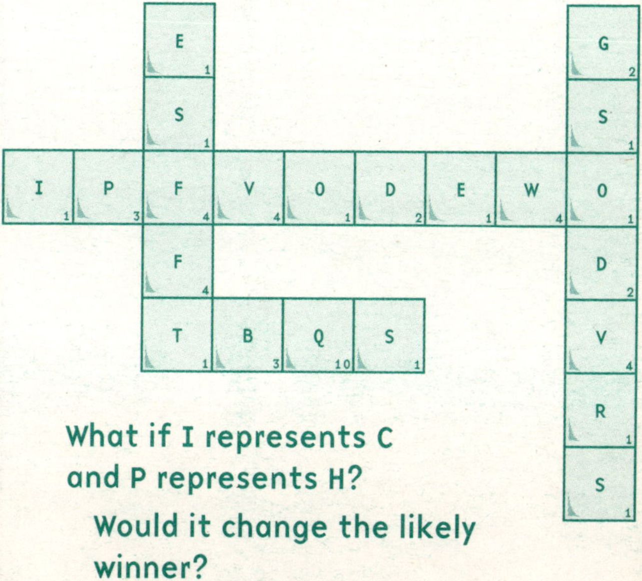

What if I represents C and P represents H?

Would it change the likely winner?

It'll certainly occupy your guests' time!

91.

Agree as a family who received the worst present and find three good reasons to love it.

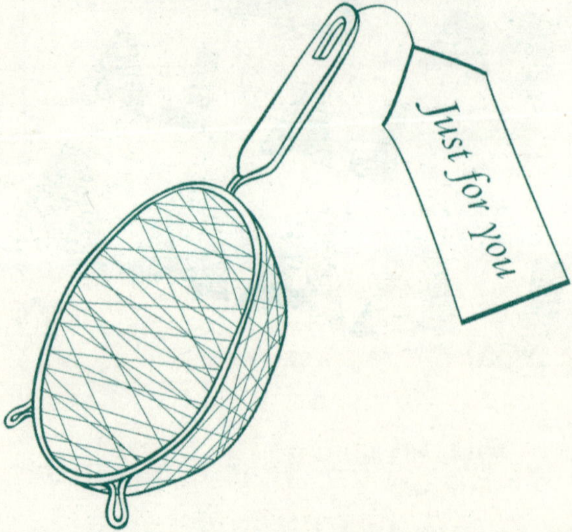

92.

Have a Christmas
sing-song.

FA LA LA LA LAAAA

Let everyone choose a number
and sing your hearts out!

93.

If it all gets too much, try this yoga pose:

Balasana

Kneel on the floor, knees hip-width apart, and lower your torso between your thighs.

Let your forehead rest on the floor and lay your hands beside your body, palms upwards.

Relax for 30 seconds. Picture each breath inhalation lifting the curve of your back.

Benefits:

- Perfect for unwinding.
- Easy to do while hiding away from other people.

94.

Feel good about all those boxes you'll be putting in the recycling.

95.

Remember the show

Stars in Their Eyes?

Regret its passing?

Stage a family re-enactment as a Christmas special.

"This Christmas, Matthew, I'm going to be..."

96.

After Christmas dinner, put all the dirty dishes in the bathtub and shut the bathroom door.

DO NOT ENTER

97.

Can you solve these Christmas cracker riddles?

All you have to do is work out the naff punchline to the joke.

1) Why are there only 25 letters in the Christmas alphabet?
2) What do you get if you cross Donald Trump with Christmas carol singers?
3) What did Adam say the day before Christmas?
4) Who is Santa's favourite singer?
5) Why can't Christmas trees knit?

6) Why is it getting harder to buy advent calendars?

7) Who hides in the bakery at Christmas?

8) What did Jack Frost say to the Snowman?

9) Who delivers presents to sharks at Christmas?

10) Why did nobody bid for Blitzen and Rudolf on eBay?

Answers overleaf

Solutions to the Christmas cracker riddles.

1) Because the angel said "Noel".

2) "O Comb Over Ye Faithful."

3) "It's Christmas Eve."

4) Elf-is Presley.

5) Because they always drop their needles.

6) Because their days are numbered.

7) A mince-spy.

8) "Have an ice day."

9) Santa Jaws.

10) Because they were two deer.

98.

How would you explain Christmas to a Martian?

Which aspects would you be proud of?

Which would make you embarrassed?

Do you think the Martian would see it as a good thing or a bad thing?

99.

Go on a family walk.

Give everyone a chocolate for each hill they climb.

100.

Read an atmospheric festive story by candlelight.

Marley was dead to begin with – there's no doubt about that. He was as dead as a doornail...

101.

Now that your
Christmas
is feeling
a lot less
stressful,
go online and
book yourself
a holiday
for the Easter weekend.